DATE			
	DISCARDED		

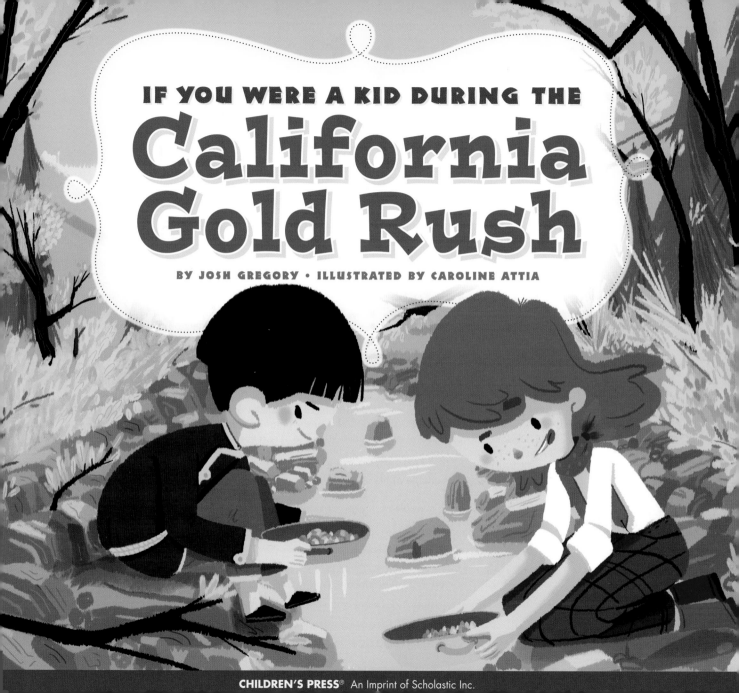

IF YOU WERE A KID DURING THE

California Gold Rush

BY JOSH GREGORY · ILLUSTRATED BY CAROLINE ATTIA

CHILDREN'S PRESS® An Imprint of Scholastic Inc.

Content Consultant
James Marten, PhD, Professor and Chair, History Department, Marquette University, Milwaukee, Wisconsin

NOTE TO THE READER, PARENT, LIBRARIAN, AND TEACHER: This book combines a historical fiction narrative with nonfiction fact boxes. While all the nonfiction fact boxes are historically accurate and true, the fiction comes solely from the imaginations of the author and illustrator.

Photos ©: 9: Radu Bercan/Shutterstock; 11: Fotosearch/Getty Images; 13: Maryann Preisinger/Dreamstime; 15: The Granger Collection; 17 left: belka_35/iStockphoto; 17 center: Warren_Price/iStockphoto; 17 right: Janet Faye Hastings/Shutterstock; 19: Science History Images/Alamy Images; 21: Bettmann/Getty Images; 23: John Elk III/ Alamy Images; 25: The Granger Collection; 27: Herbert Gehr/The LIFE Picture Collection/Getty Images.

Library of Congress Cataloging-in-Publication Data
Names: Gregory, Josh, author. | Attia, Caroline, illustrator.
Title: If you were a kid during the California Gold Rush / by Josh Gregory ; illustrated by Caroline Attia.
Description: New York : Children's Press, an imprint of Scholastic Inc., [2018] | Series: If you were a kid | Includes bibliographical references and index.
Identifiers: LCCN 2017032485 | ISBN 9780531232149 (library binding) | ISBN 9780531243121 (pbk.)
Subjects: LCSH: California—Gold discoveries—Juvenile literature. | California—History—1846-1850—Juvenile literature. | Frontier and pioneer life—California—Juvenile literature.
Classification: LCC F865 .G745 2018 | DDC 979.4/04—dc23
LC record available at https://lccn.loc.gov/2017032485

Scholastic Inc., 557 Broadway, New York, NY 10012

1 2 3 4 5 6 7 8 9 10 R 27 26 25 24 23 22 21 20 19 18

TABLE OF CONTENTS

4

A Different Way of Life

On January 24, 1848, a carpenter named James Marshall was working to build a **sawmill** on California's American River. He noticed something sparkling in the water and soon realized that it was gold! News of Marshall's discovery spread through newspapers and word of mouth. This kicked off an era known as the Gold Rush. Thousands of people from around the world hurried to California. They hoped to get rich by finding gold. Most were men who left their families behind in a race to gather gold as quickly as they could. As the Gold Rush went on, many of the **prospectors'** families traveled to California to join them.

Turn the page to set off on your own Gold Rush adventure! You will see that life today is a lot different than it was in the past.

Meet Louise!

Louise Cooper and her mother have recently moved from Illinois to a mining town in California. They came to be with Louise's father and older brother, who have been prospecting for gold. The two men had done well during their first few weeks in California. They sometimes made hundreds of dollars in a single day. Unfortunately, they have not been finding as much gold lately. Food is expensive. Their money is running out. Louise is still hopeful, but things are getting tough for the family . . .

Meet Feng!

Li Feng came to California with his father and uncle all the way from China. They sailed more than 5,000 miles (8,047 kilometers) across the Pacific Ocean to get there. Like others, they originally planned to make it rich as gold prospectors. But instead, they have had greater success selling supplies to miners. Feng still wants to look for gold, though. He thinks the chance of getting rich quick is way more exciting than helping to run the family business . . .

"Isn't there anything left to eat?" Louise asked. Her stomach was still growling after her very small breakfast.

"Sorry," her mom answered. "We have to save the rest for later in case your father and brother don't find any gold today. We don't have any money left to buy more food."

Louise sighed. She thought the move to California would make her family rich. But so far, it wasn't working.

8

GOING OUT WEST

For most people, getting to California was a very long journey. Many Americans came from the East Coast. They had to sail south all the way around South America and back up to California! Others took a shortcut across Panama in Central America. People coming from the Midwest usually traveled by land in covered wagons.

KEY

- Overland route; 4–6 months
- Panama route; 3-5 months
- Cape Horn route; 6–8 months

San Francisco
Boston
St. Joseph
Panama
Cape Horn

9

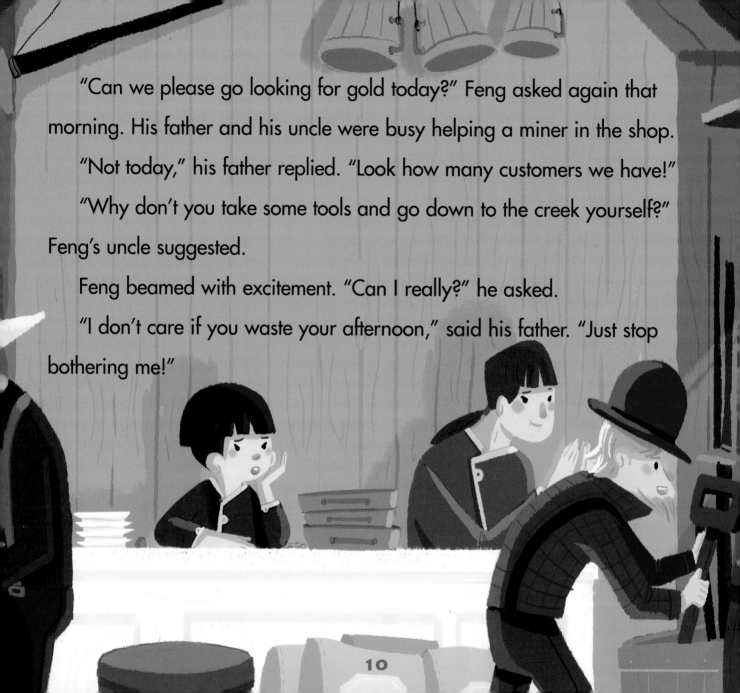

"Can we please go looking for gold today?" Feng asked again that morning. His father and his uncle were busy helping a miner in the shop.

"Not today," his father replied. "Look how many customers we have!"

"Why don't you take some tools and go down to the creek yourself?" Feng's uncle suggested.

Feng beamed with excitement. "Can I really?" he asked.

"I don't care if you waste your afternoon," said his father. "Just stop bothering me!"

10

BUILDING A BUSINESS

Not everyone who traveled to California during the Gold Rush became a miner. The area's population was growing, and businesses were needed to serve everyone. Some of California's new residents found great success selling supplies to miners. Some opened restaurants. Many of these business owners made more money than the average prospector.

Levi Strauss came to San Francisco in 1853 and later became famous by manufacturing and selling the first metal-riveted denim jeans. Here, two gold miners wear Levi's jeans in 1882.

Later that morning, Louise was watching her dad and brother pan for gold. She had expected it to be fun and exciting. But after coming to California, she had learned that it was hard, boring work. Worst of all, they hadn't found a single bit of gold all morning.

"I'm going for a walk in the woods," Louise announced.

"Sure, sure," her dad mumbled, without looking up from his work. "Be sure you're back by dinnertime."

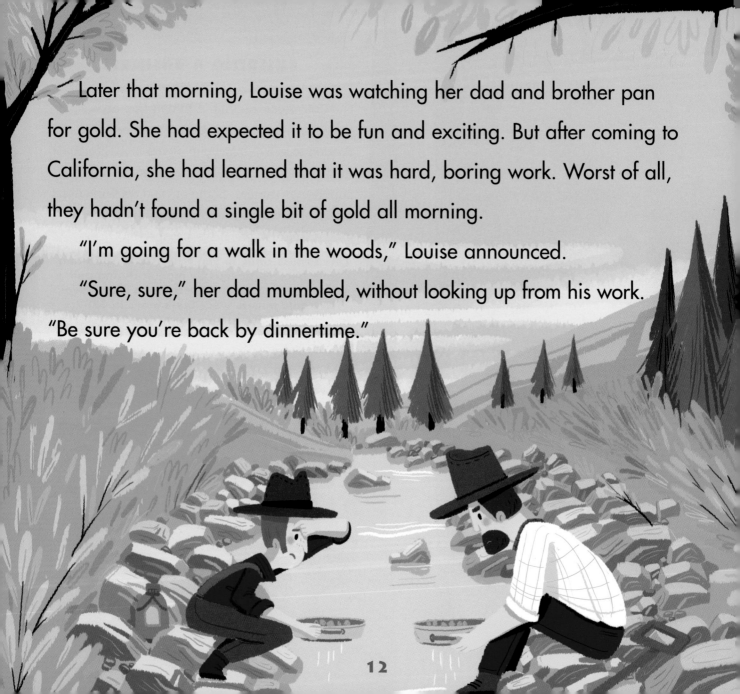

TOOLS OF THE TRADE

Prospectors used many tools and **techniques** to collect gold. The simplest way was called panning. A miner would collect water, gravel, and soil from a river or creek in a pan. He would then swirl the pan so the water and other materials would spill over the sides. That would leave the heavier gold at the bottom. A miner might repeat this process up to 50 times each day. And he might only get a little bit of gold. Another common method involved setting up a box by the river or creek. It would be filled with water and materials. Then it was rocked back and forth to separate out the gold.

Miners used pickaxes to break apart rocks and soil as they worked.

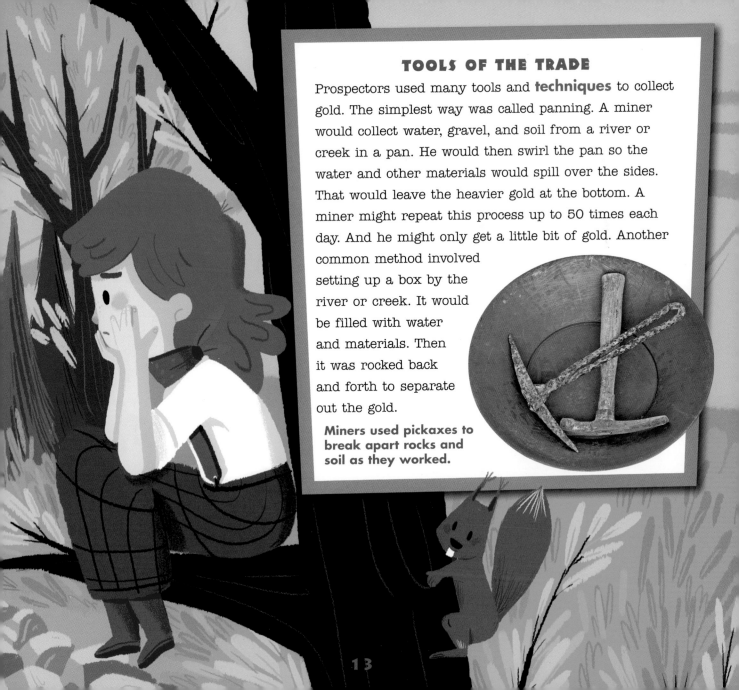

"Good luck!" Feng's uncle said with a chuckle. "You're going to need it. Look how many people are out looking for gold. None of them are getting rich."

"I know," Feng answered. "But I'm bored of working here every day." He placed a pan and some snacks in a bag and headed out the door. His uncle shrugged and shook his head.

COMING TO AMERICA

During the Gold Rush, many **immigrants** came to California in hopes of getting rich. People from China joined the Gold Rush in especially large numbers. In 1849, there were 54 Chinese people living in California. By 1876, there were 116,000!

Chinese children walk through San Francisco's Chinatown sometime around 1900.

Louise was walking through the woods. Suddenly, she heard a noise in front of her. A boy popped out from behind a tree. She jumped back, surprised.

"Hi," the boy said. "I'm Feng!"

"You scared me!" Louise exclaimed.

She introduced herself, and the two decided to look for gold together. Soon, they came to a creek. Feng offered to share his snacks with Louise. She was very grateful for something to eat. Afterward, she bent down to drink from the creek.

"There's something sparkling here!" she yelled. "I think I found gold!"

WHAT'S FOR LUNCH?

During the Gold Rush, most people relied on simple meals. The meals needed to be prepared and eaten quickly. People did not want to take long breaks from looking for gold. Sourdough bread was very popular. Some miners purchased foods such as bacon and beans from stores. Others hunted wild animals for meat. Fruits and vegetables were very hard to come by. This caused many people to come down with **scurvy**.

"I can't believe it!" Louise said. "My family is going to be so excited."

"Quiet!" Feng warned. "If other miners hear, they'll show up. Then they'll take all the gold for themselves."

Louise promised to be more careful. The two friends collected as much gold as they could with Feng's tools. But it was getting dark. They split up their shares and agreed to meet at Feng's the next day.

A DIFFICULT LIFE

Mining for gold was hard, dangerous work. All kinds of injuries were common, from cuts to broken bones. There were often no doctors around to help wounded miners. Disease was another big problem. More than half of all miners were **infected** with hookworms. These worms dug into the feet of people with worn-out boots. Some people had no boots at all. Miners also got sick from drinking unclean water. People tended to live very close to one another and had poor **hygiene**. Sicknesses spread easily among them.

Miners got dirty, sweaty, and wet as they worked all day.

Louise couldn't wait to show her family her gold. They stared in surprise as she revealed it.

"We're saved!" her mom exclaimed.

Everyone started discussing plans to gather more gold at Louise's spot the next day.

"Don't forget about Feng," Louise said. "It's his gold, too."

Thinking hard, her dad rubbed his chin. "Well," he said, "I guess that's true."

HOME SWEET HOME

When the Gold Rush began, newly arrived miners had nowhere to live. They often slept outdoors or in quickly built shacks. Over time, these early camps grew to become towns. People built houses, stores, and other buildings. Some even built simple hotels where miners could pay to sleep in a bed. But these buildings were far from fancy. People often had to deal with leaky roofs, rats, and other problems.

Mining camps often became bustling towns full of people and activity.

Feng got up early the next morning
and started gathering his tools.

"Where are you going?" his father asked. "You had
your fun yesterday. Today, you need to stay and work."

Slowly, Feng pulled a handkerchief from his pocket
and unwrapped it.

"Is that what I think it is?" his father asked.

Feng nodded. "I know where to get more, too."

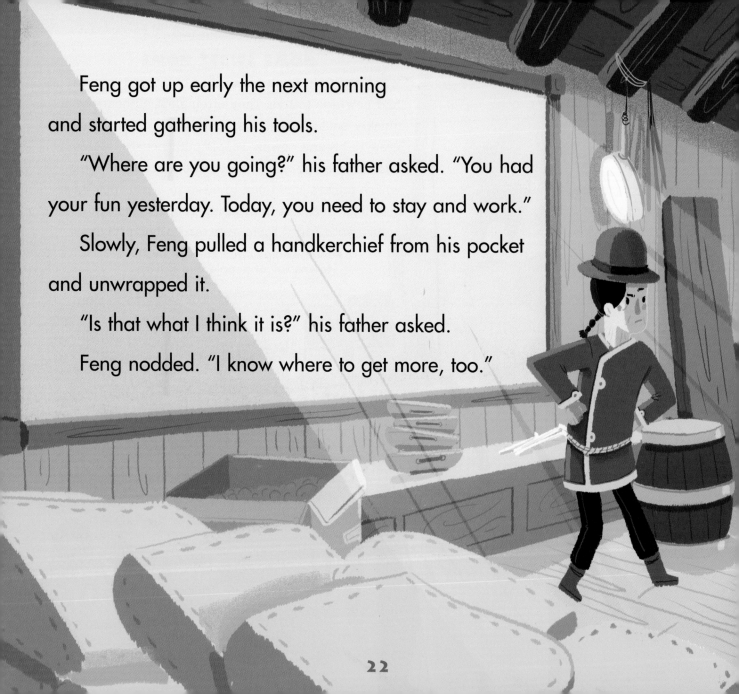

AN $80 EGG?

As the Gold Rush went on, supplies started to become very expensive. There were few farms in California. Food had to be brought in from other states. But too many people were moving to California. There wasn't enough food to go around. Merchants raised their prices as high as they could. A single egg could cost $3 in 1851. That would be more than $80 in today's money!

Stores in gold rush towns sold everything from food to mining tools.

Just then, Louise arrived at the store with her dad and brother. Feng's father demanded that they show him where the gold was. Louise's father refused. The adults started arguing about who had a right to the gold.

"Stop!" yelled Louise. "There's plenty for all of us."

"Yeah," said Feng as he pointed out the window. "And people are starting to pay attention to all the shouting."

With that, everyone got much quieter. They started planning how to collect the gold together.

THE ORIGINAL CALIFORNIANS

Prospectors were not the first people to come to California. When the Gold Rush began, Native Americans had been living in the area for a long time. Prospectors and other settlers took control of the Native Americans' land. They either killed the natives, forced them to leave, or made them work. Between 1845 and 1870, California's Native American population went from 150,000 to 30,000.

California's Native Americans suffered greatly as a result of the Gold Rush.

They needed to stop other miners from following them. So everyone took different paths to the gold. Louise's dad and brother were experienced miners. Feng's family had the latest tools. They worked all day and collected more gold than they could have imagined.

"This is amazing," said Louise's dad. "We're going to have so much money from this gold. You can have seconds at breakfast every day now, Louise!"

"Just wait," said Louise. "You haven't seen anything yet."

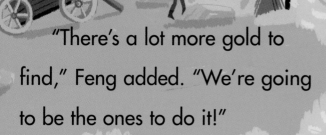

"There's a lot more gold to find," Feng added. "We're going to be the ones to do it!"

THE END OF AN ERA

By the end of the 1850s, prospectors had found most of the gold that was easy to reach. More gold was buried deeper underground. Collecting that gold required powerful **hydraulic** equipment. Individual gold miners were not able to do this kind of work. They were soon replaced by large mining companies. It was the end of an era.

California gold miners relied more and more on heavy machinery in the decades following the Gold Rush.

California During the Gold Rush

During the Gold Rush, cities such as San Francisco and Sacramento grew rapidly as miners flooded into the region. Most gold discoveries took place in the area between the Sierra Nevada mountains along California's eastern border and the Sacramento and San Joaquin Rivers.

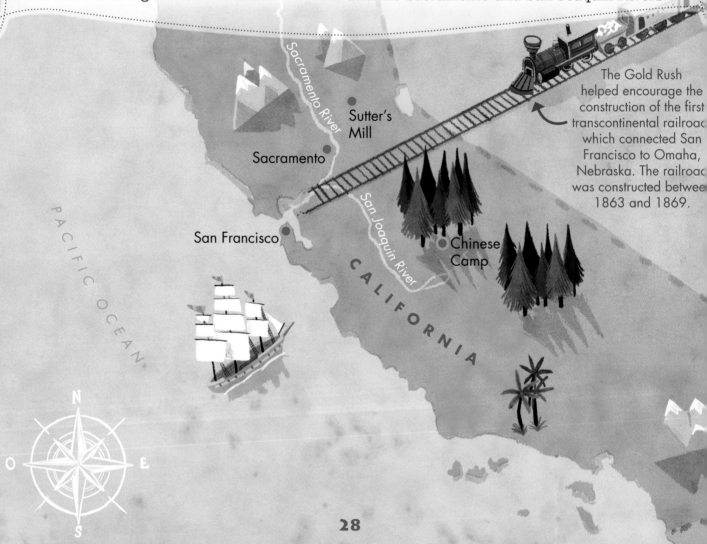

The Gold Rush helped encourage the construction of the first transcontinental railroad which connected San Francisco to Omaha, Nebraska. The railroad was constructed between 1863 and 1869.

Sacramento River

Sutter's Mill

Sacramento

San Joaquin River

San Francisco

PACIFIC OCEAN

Chinese Camp

CALIFORNIA

Timeline

1846 The Native American population of California is about 150,000. The non-native population is about 7,600 to 8,000.

January 24, 1848 The Gold Rush kicks off when a man named James Marshall discovers gold at Sutter's Mill.

February 2, 1848 The United States takes control of California after a war with Mexico.

April 1, 1848 Newspapers are sent out from California announcing the gold discovery.

September 9, 1850 California becomes the 31st state.

1852 At the peak of the Gold Rush, about $80 million worth of gold is collected in California. This would be worth about $2 billion in today's money.

1860 At the conclusion of the Gold Rush, California's official state population is about 380,000.

1870 California's Native American population has dropped to about 30,000.

Words to Know

hydraulic (hye-DRAW-lik) describing machines that work on power created by liquid moving through pipes under pressure

hygiene (HYE-jeen) the practice of keeping yourself and the things around you clean in order to stay healthy

immigrants (IM-i-gruhnts) people who move from one country to another and settle there

infected (in-FEKT-id) carrying germs or viruses that cause disease

prospectors (PRAH-spek-turz) people who are in search of something, such as gold

sawmill (SAW-mil) a place where people use machines to saw logs into lumber

scurvy (SKUR-vee) a disease caused by a lack of vitamin C

techniques (tek-NEEKS) ways of doing something that require skill

Index

ABOUT THE AUTHOR

Josh Gregory is the author of more than 120 books for kids. He has written about everything from animals to technology to history. A graduate of the University of Missouri–Columbia, he currently lives in Chicago, Illinois.

ABOUT THE ILLUSTRATOR

Caroline Attia is an award-winning illustrator and animator. She graduated from the École nationale supérieure des Arts Décoratifs (ENSAD) in Paris, where she directed her first short film, *Tango on Saw*. She works from her studio in Montreuil, France.

Visit this Scholastic website for more information about the California Gold Rush:

www.factsfornow.scholastic.com
Enter the keywords **Gold Rush**